Life Goes On...

Also by the Authors
Life is Too Short . . . (with Helen Bland)

Life Goes On...

Patti Falzarano, Bo Niles, and Mary Sears

WARNER BOOKS

A Time Warner Company

Copyright © 1996 by Patti Falzarano, Bo Niles, and Mary Sears

Warner Books, Inc., 1271 Avenue of the Americas, New York, NY 10020
Visit our web site at http://pathfinder.com/twep

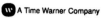 A Time Warner Company

Printed in the United States of America
First Printing: July 1996
10 9 8 7 6 5 4 3 2 1

Library of Congress Cataloging-in-Publication Data

Falzarano, Patti.
    Life goes on-- / Patti Falzarano, Bo Niles, and Mary Sears.
      p.   cm.
    Continues: Life is too short--.
    ISBN: 0-446-67079-0
    1. Life--Humor. 2. American wit and humor. I. Niles, Bo.
II. Sears, Mary. III. Life is too short—. IV. Title.
PN6231.L48F35 1996   95-41995
818' .5402—dc20   CIP

Book design by H. Roberts
Cover design by Julia Kushnirsky
Cover illustration by Merle Nacht

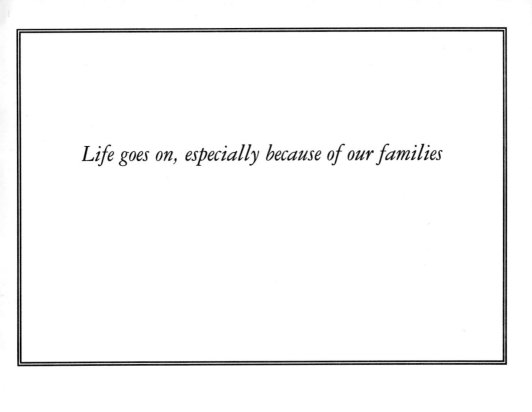

Life goes on, especially because of our families

Life Goes On...

LIFE GOES ON . . .

Especially

- ❏ when you can't stop laughing
- ❏ with the wind in your sails
- ❏ without humidity
- ❏ when the deer don't eat your flowers

LIFE GOES ON . . .

Even when
- ❏ the applause dies down
- ❏ you don't get the lead
- ❏ your half of the two-man costume falls off
- ❏ your bathing suit comes off in the waves
- ❏ he/she is younger and better looking

LIFE GOES ON . . .

Even

- ❏ when you join the health club and never go
- ❏ with toilet tissue stuck to your shoe
- ❏ when the kids' sneakers cost more than your shoes
- ❏ when you're wearing your navy blue blazer and they think you're an usher

LIFE GOES ON . . .

Even when you've dropped
- ❑ a stitch
- ❑ the ball
- ❑ a hint that was ignored

LIFE GOES ON . . .

Even when you break
- ❑ a nail
- ❑ a glass
- ❑ a promise you really couldn't keep

LIFE GOES ON . . .

Especially when
❏ your friend gives you tickets
❏ the kids next door grow up
❏ you're met at the airport
❏ you're inspired

LIFE GOES ON . . .

Even when
- ❏ the alarm clock doesn't
- ❏ your candidate doesn't
- ❏ your wardrobe doesn't
- ❏ your memory doesn't

LIFE GOES ON . . .

Even when you could use
- ❏ a face lift
- ❏ a tummy tuck
- ❏ hormones

LIFE GOES ON . . .

Even when you lose
- ❑ your way
- ❑ your cool
- ❑ a filling

LIFE GOES ON . . .

Even when
- ❏ the raccoons raid the garbage
- ❏ the cat eats the goldfish
- ❏ the squirrels move in
- ❏ you've got bats in your belfry

LIFE GOES ON . . .

Especially when
❑ there's no one in line ahead of you
❑ the aspirin kicks in
❑ they hug you without asking

LIFE GOES ON . . .

Especially

- ❏ after a good night's sleep
- ❏ when the tough get going
- ❏ with chocolate chips

LIFE GOES ON . . .

Even when

❏ your skirt has static cling
❏ your dress is longer than your raincoat
❏ you forgot to cut off the tags
❏ your hem droops

LIFE GOES ON . . .

Even
- ❑ with a bad perm
- ❑ when your roots show
- ❑ when your best friend moves away—and your hairstylist does, too

LIFE GOES ON . . .

Even

❏ when you forgot to clean the paintbrush
❏ after your helium balloon gets away
❏ after your cherub has a tantrum in the mall

LIFE GOES ON . . .

Even

- ❏ when TV newscasters no longer look old
- ❏ though the kids now ski faster than you
- ❏ when scary rides become hazardous to your health instead of just scary

Life Goes On . . .

Especially when

❏ the drive-in teller sends back a lollipop
❏ the egg whites form peaks
❏ you get to lick the bowl—and both beaters

LIFE GOES ON . . .

Especially when
- ❏ you get a high five

  and

Even when
- ❏ you've been dealt a bad hand

LIFE GOES ON . . .

Especially when
❑ you agree to disagree
    and
Even when
❑ you agree to disagree

LIFE GOES ON . . .

Even

- ❏ in a heat wave
- ❏ on the bottom bunk
- ❏ when practice begins at five in the morning

LIFE GOES ON . . .

Even when

❑ the check bounces

❑ the ATM is Temporarily Out of Service

❑ you're last in line

LIFE GOES ON . . .

Even

- ❏ though the turkey didn't thaw
- ❏ when you're out of milk
- ❏ when the grill runs out of fuel in the middle of your burgers

Life Goes On . . .

Even

- ❏ when the cast has to stay on for six more weeks
- ❏ when the retainer goes into the cafeteria's garbage again
- ❏ when you have to be in the talent show
- ❏ when the homework doesn't get done
- ❏ with a curfew

LIFE GOES ON . . .

Especially when
- ❏ your attitude changes
- ❏ you get the promotion
- ❏ your cholesterol goes down

LIFE GOES ON . . .

Even when
- ❏ your luggage doesn't have wheels
- ❏ your plane is rerouted
- ❏ there's turbulence

LIFE GOES ON . . .

Even when
- [ ] the temperature plunges
- [ ] the plow leaves a wall of snow at the end of your driveway

    and

Especially when
- [ ] you're on the beach and it's snowing back home

LIFE GOES ON . . .

Even when
- ❏ your kids move back home
- ❏ carpenter ants move in . . . and your mother-in-law does, too

27

LIFE GOES ON . . .

Even when
- ❏ you run out of time
- ❏ you run up the phone bill
- ❏ you run new pantyhose
- ❏ you're running on empty

LIFE GOES ON . . .

Especially when
- ❏ you carry the torch
- ❏ you set them on fire
- ❏ you see an old flame

LIFE GOES ON . . .

Even when you have
- ❏ a hangnail
- ❏ a paper cut
- ❏ a sty in your eye

30

LIFE GOES ON . . .

Even when
- ❏ your nose runs
- ❏ your feet swell
- ❏ your back aches
- ❏ your waistband's too tight

LIFE GOES ON . . .

Even

- ❏ when the bridge is out
- ❏ with construction for the next five miles
- ❏ when the drive-up window is closed and you have to walk inside

LIFE GOES ON . . .

Even when
- ❑ it's not what it was cracked up to be
- ❑ the bonbon looks good on the outside . . .
  but it's yucky on the inside

LIFE GOES ON . . .

Especially when

- ❏ your team is undefeated
- ❏ you catch a trout on your own fly
- ❏ you don't have to parallel park

LIFE GOES ON . . .

Especially when
- ❏ you get what it's worth
- ❏ you come from behind
- ❏ you win the lottery

LIFE GOES ON . . .

Especially
❏ when the soufflé rises
and

Even
❏ after it falls

LIFE GOES ON . . .

Especially
- ❏ after early retirement
  and

Even
- ❏ after early retirement

LIFE GOES ON . . .

Even when
- ❏ deciphering airfare rules and regulations
- ❏ the plane leaves the gate on time and then sits on the runway
- ❏ you wake up with your head on the shoulder of the passenger sitting next to you

LIFE GOES ON . . .

Even when it rains on
- ❏ your vacation
- ❏ your parade
- ❏ your newly washed car

LIFE GOES ON . . .

Even when

- ❏ your ring turns green a week after the wedding
- ❏ something red turns the whole wash pink
- ❏ a bird nests in the clothes-dryer vent

LIFE GOES ON . . .

Even when
- ❏ your favorite sweater gets the fuzzies
- ❏ the baby cries all night
- ❏ the whole family gets the flu

LIFE GOES ON . . .

Even after
- ☐ the waterbed leaks
- ☐ April 15th
- ☐ the audit

LIFE GOES ON . . .

Especially when
- ☐ you beat your own best time
- ☐ you get the last available tickets
- ☐ you're treated like royalty

LIFE GOES ON . . .

Even when

- ❏ you forgot to record the check
- ❏ someone takes the parking place you've been waiting for
- ❏ the wind blows the leaf pile back onto your lawn

LIFE GOES ON . . .

Even when
- ❏ the canoe tips over
- ❏ the hamster gets away
- ❏ the rug has fleas
- ❏ the guinea pig has a weight problem

LIFE GOES ON . . .

Even when you have
- ❑ a zit
- ❑ a canker sore
- ❑ a bad hair day
- ❑ wrinkles, rather than character lines

LIFE GOES ON . . .

Even without
- ❏ butter
- ❏ reservations
- ❏ exact change
- ❏ your umbrella and rain shoes

Life Goes On . . .

Especially when

❏ you don't give up
❏ you know the ropes
❏ you know when to back off
❏ you ace it

LIFE GOES ON . . .

Even when they
- ❏ cancel your favorite show
- ❏ discontinue your favorite shade of lipstick
- ❏ stop making your favorite bra
- ❏ fold your favorite magazine

LIFE GOES ON . . .

Even after you get
- ❏ braces
- ❏ reading glasses
- ❏ arch supports

LIFE GOES ON . . .

Even when
- ❏ your heel breaks
- ❏ your heart breaks
- ❏ you have to break in new shoes

LIFE GOES ON . . .

Even

- ❑ when you realize you've walked around with the back of your blouse undone
- ❑ when the "charming getaway" is not what you expected
- ❑ in the funniest places

LIFE GOES ON . . .

Especially
- ❏ on weekends
- ❏ when you practice
- ❏ when you're in love

LIFE GOES ON . . .

Even when
- ❏ you get bumped from your flight
  and

Especially when
- ❏ you get bumped up to first class

54

Life Goes On . . .

Even

❑ during the scary parts
❑ with subtitles
❑ in spite of the fine print

LIFE GOES ON . . .

Even
- ❏ when your socks don't match
- ❏ when you forgot to pack underwear
- ❏ after the night before

LIFE GOES ON . . .

Even when
- ❏ the warranty runs out
- ❏ the battery runs down
- ❏ they give you the runaround

LIFE GOES ON . . .

Even when you run out of
- ❏ gas
- ❏ steam
- ❏ shaving cream
- ❏ film
- ❏ floss
- ❏ ink
- ❏ patience
- ❏ ideas

Life Goes On . . .

Especially when

- ❏ a rainbow crosses your path
- ❏ the crocuses come up
- ❏ the estimate matches the bill

LIFE GOES ON . . .

Especially when

- ❏ you get it right the first time
- ❏ your sunflowers soar twelve feet high
- ❏ you find a movie the whole family can enjoy

LIFE GOES ON . . .

Even

- ❏ after bridgework
- ❏ when you sit on your glasses
- ❏ when you thicken/sag in places you didn't expect
- ❏ when you get a gutter ball

LIFE GOES ON . . .

Even when
- ❏ the market is soft
- ❏ the computers are down
- ❏ the mosquitoes are out
- ❏ the jig is up

Life Goes On . . .

Even when

- ❏ your neighbors feel "what's yours is mine"
- ❏ you're the only one who picks up dirty clothes
- ❏ they couldn't care less

Life Goes On . . .

Even when
- ❏ your elastic gives out
- ❏ your shoelace breaks
- ❏ your blind date seems hopeless from minute one

LIFE GOES ON . . .

Especially when

- ❑ the doctor says, "No shots!"
- ❑ the dentist says, "No cavities!"
- ❑ the boss says, "Good job!"

LIFE GOES ON . . .

Even when
- ❏ the seltzer is flat
- ❏ the bananas are black
- ❏ the lettuce is limp
- ❏ the brown sugar is hard as a brick
- ❏ you've got RB-on-rye stuck between your teeth

Life Goes On . . .

Even

- [ ] when you give up the hit
- [ ] when you're a bench warmer
- [ ] in the dugout
- [ ] in the cheap seats

LIFE GOES ON . . .

Even when
❏ the car dies
❏ you can't get your money back
❏ it wasn't what you ordered
❏ they take you for a ride

LIFE GOES ON . . .

Even when you
- ☐ strike out
- ☐ break up
- ☐ fall down

LIFE GOES ON . . .

Especially when you
- ❏ break a deuce
- ❏ hit a hole in one
- ❏ hike/bike to the top

LIFE GOES ON . . .

Even when the kids
- ❏ go to camp
- ❏ go to college

and

Especially when they
- ❏ go to bed

LIFE GOES ON . . .

Even after

- ❏ you've locked the keys in the car
- ❏ your bicycle chain slips off
- ❏ the odometer rolls over
- ❏ you have to stand on the bus all the way home

Life Goes On . . .

Even when
- ❏ you snore on the train
- ❏ your roommate snores
- ❏ your own snoring keeps you awake

LIFE GOES ON . . .

Even after you get a spot on your
- ❏ tie
- ❏ new dress
- ❏ favorite tablecloth
- ❏ carpet
- ❏ reputation

Life Goes On . . .

Even

- ☐ with hayfever
- ☐ without TV
- ☐ unplugged
- ☐ in row W

LIFE GOES ON . . .

Especially when
- ❏ the "lightbulb" goes on
- ❏ the wallpaper seams match
- ❏ the paint dries the same color as the paint chip

LIFE GOES ON . . .

Especially when
- ❏ everyone agrees
- ❏ you get flowers
- ❏ you make the deadline

LIFE GOES ON . . .

Especially when you
- ❏ conquer a challenge
- ❏ pick a winner
- ❏ get a refund

LIFE GOES ON . . .

Even when
- ❏ you do things the hard way
- ❏ you hit the rapids
- ❏ they don't think it's funny
- ❏ the joke's on you

LIFE GOES ON . . .

Even when your boss
- ❑ nods off during your presentation
- ❑ laughs when you ask for a raise
- ❑ sees you at the health club when you've called in sick

LIFE GOES ON . . .

Even when
   ❏ the electricity goes off
      and
Especially when
   ❏ it goes back on

LIFE GOES ON . . .

Even when
- [ ] he/she doesn't phone

  and

Especially when
- [ ] he/she does

LIFE GOES ON . . .

Even when you can't remember
- ❏ the steps
- ❏ the words
- ❏ your PIN
- ❏ your long-distance access code

LIFE GOES ON . . .

Even when you miss
- ❏ the point
- ❏ the mark
- ❏ the bus
- ❏ the exit
- ❏ an appointment
- ❏ your flight
- ❏ your mother

LIFE GOES ON . . .

Especially
- ❏ in the spring
- ❏ on a sunny day
- ❏ after high school

LIFE GOES ON . . .

Even when
- ❏ the pop-up thermometer doesn't
- ❏ the easy-open top isn't
- ❏ the spray nozzle won't

LIFE GOES ON . . .

Especially when
❏ you hear the ice cream truck bells
and
Even when
❏ the ice cream falls out of the cone

LIFE GOES ON . . .

Even

- ❏ during long car rides with the family
- ❏ with sibling rivalry
- ❏ when your baby-sitter goes to college

LIFE GOES ON . . .

Even when
- ❏ you're locked out
- ❏ you're stood up
- ❏ you're late again
- ❏ they breathe down your neck

LIFE GOES ON . . .

Especially

❏ when you lend a hand
❏ when the alpine slide turns out to be fun
❏ with pecs and a six-pack
❏ with hot fudge

Life Goes On . . .

Even after
❏ they've all grown up
and
Especially after
❏ they've all grown up

Life Goes On . . .

Even when

❑ you get in the shower and there's no soap

and

Even when

❑ you get out of the shower and there's no towel

LIFE GOES ON . . .

Even when

❑ you can't remember the "special" place you put something so it won't get lost

❑ the math is beyond you

❑ you can't wear a bikini anymore

LIFE GOES ON . . .

Especially when
- ❏ they remember your birthday

and

Especially when
- ❏ they forget your birthday

LIFE GOES ON . . .

Even when
- ❏ the shower leaks
- ❏ the crayon melts
- ❏ you have to clean up

LIFE GOES ON . . .

Even when
- ❏ the fire goes out and you're out of matches
- ❏ winter just won't quit
- ❏ you're snowed in with three kids and no videos

LIFE GOES ON . . .

Especially when
- ❏ you've gone that extra mile
- ❏ they've all had chicken pox
- ❏ you think of the right thing to say

LIFE GOES ON . . .

Even after
   ❑ you leave
      and
Especially after
   ❑ you leave

LIFE GOES ON . . .

Even

- ❏ when the monarchy doesn't
- ❏ after your lease expires
- ❏ without the right stuff
- ❏ when management is inept
- ❏ when you have to shut up

LIFE GOES ON . . .

Even

- ☐ when your bangs are way too short
- ☐ with chipped nail polish
- ☐ when they cut instead of trimmed

LIFE GOES ON . . .

Even when your computer
- ❏ develops a virus
- ❏ crashes—and you forgot to save
- ❏ changes fonts in midstream

LIFE GOES ON . . .

Even when

❑ someone steps on your new white sneakers

❑ you forgot to use moth balls

❑ your tennis racket pops a string

❑ your mate goes to Paris on a business trip—
and you don't

LIFE GOES ON . . .

Especially when
- ❏ you win in Las Vegas
- ❏ your game is below par
- ❏ you finish early
- ❏ you finish first
- ❏ you finish the whole thing

LIFE GOES ON . . .

Even when
   ❏ you lose track of time
      and
Especially when
   ❏ you lose track of time

LIFE GOES ON . . .

Even when
❏ you do it yourself
and
Especially when
❏ you do it yourself

LIFE GOES ON . . .

Even when
- ❏ old friends don't recognize you
    and
Especially when
- ❏ old friends don't recognize you

Life Goes On . . .

Even when
- ❏ you start going bald, gray—or both
- ❏ you gain weight on the new diet
- ❏ the other guy wins

Life Goes On . . .

Even when

- ❏ your job requires a hairnet
- ❏ your jeans won't button
- ❏ you rock the boat

LIFE GOES ON . . .

Even when
- ❏ the cards don't stack up
- ❏ it's no longer considered baby fat
- ❏ someone else is wearing "your" outfit

Life Goes On . . .

Especially when you
- ❏ land on your feet
- ❏ land the big one
- ❏ land the job you've been hoping for

LIFE GOES ON . . .

Even

- ❏ when you're out of ice
- ❏ without mittens
- ❏ when daylight savings time ends
- ❏ when the cat/gerbil/rabbit has another litter

LIFE GOES ON . . .

Even when
- ❏ the bagel burns
- ❏ the crème brûlée turns to charcoal
- ❏ the omelet sticks to the pan
- ❏ the ice cream melts before you get home

LIFE GOES ON . . .

Even when

❏ you can't remember his/her name anymore
   and

Especially when

❏ you can't remember his/her name anymore

LIFE GOES ON . . .

Even when
- ❏ everything goes wrong
  and

Especially when
- ❏ everything goes right

LIFE GOES ON . . .

And so do some
- ☐ meetings
- ☐ evenings
- ☐ parties
- ☐ relationships

Life Goes On . . .

And so do
- ❏ good times
- ❏ good friends
- ❏ good memories

and so must the show

LIFE GOES ON . . .

Even after
- [ ] 30
- [ ] 40
- [ ] 50

and especially after
- [ ] 60
- [ ] 70
- [ ] 80
- [ ] 90

and incredibly after 100!

LIFE GOES ON . . .

and on . . .